IN SEARCH OF JAI
"MR KIRK OF BI

Ailish D'A

One evening in about 1912, two young men .... _
enquiries about a Nottinghamshire author, whom they admired, and
eventually found the cottage on The Banks where James Prior lived.

> *'They knocked at the door, and a romantic interview took place, James
> Prior standing on his doorstep outlined against a dim light that came
> from the house, and they, declining his invitation to enter, standing in
> the outer darkness. They told him they honoured him and were grateful
> to him for having written such books as "Forest Folk" and "A Walking
> Gentleman". He told them they were the first men to come to his door
> for that purpose, and he thanked them. A few quick words, a pressure of
> hands, and they were away, leaving behind no clue to their identity. But
> they had seen and heard enough to make their hearts beat with pride yet
> burn with indignation. They had found a man who was not only a genius
> but a fine spirit; and they had found him unhonoured, unrewarded, no
> longer young, no longer hopeful, yet bravely accepting what seemed to
> him then, a final discouragement.'[1]*

One of them was Stephen Fisher, who subsequently returned and became
'closest and dearest friend' with the author. Most of the biographical
details we have about James Prior come to us from Stephen Fisher, a
young lawyer and fan of Prior's books, who became his friend and
champion. He was active in trying to bring Prior's work back to public
notice, and after Prior's death set up The James Prior Memorial
Committee. He supplied biographical information to Robert Mellors for
'Men of Nottingham and Nottinghamshire' (1924), and all subsequent
accounts seem to rely heavily on Fisher's details.

My interest in James Prior began by chance. As we all emerged from the
Covid pandemic I needed incentives to get me out of the house and back
into the world. One day the 'Inspire' brochure dropped through the letter
box. Leafing through it over a cup of coffee, I noticed a four-week course
at the West Bridgford Library, 'Exploring Literary Locations'. It would fit
into a spare afternoon and was an easy bus ride away, so I signed up. It
turned out to be a truly 'inspired' decision. The course was delivered by
John Smith and was based on his book, writing as John Baird, *Follow the*

Moon and the Stars: A Literary Journey through Nottinghamshire, published by Five Leaves in Nottingham in 2021. At the first session we all introduced ourselves and hearing that I lived in Bingham, John said that there was an author who had lived in Bingham at the end of the 19th century. I was intrigued and puzzled that neither I nor any of my 'booky' friends had heard of him before. So began an investigation to see what more could be discovered about this apparently largely forgotten author and his connections with Bingham.

Starting with Fisher, I consulted census records, County and City Archives and began to track down copies of Prior's books, some at Bromley House Library and some through hours of searching on the internet. Gradually a fuller picture emerged of a remarkable man, a poet, novelist, a collector of local dialect, a warm-hearted husband and father who suffered tragedies and disappointment in his declining years. With a renewal of interest in Nottinghamshire's literary heritage, thanks largely to the Nottingham UNESCO City of Literature organisation, it is time to bring Prior and his work back to a wider audience.

BEGINNINGS

James Prior Kirk was born on 9th September 1851 in the city of Nottingham, at a house on Mapperley Road. His mother was Sarah Jane Prior, one of four sisters, who grew up on Derby Road, Nottingham. She married James Kirk in 1848 and they had five children, three daughters and two sons: Mary Louisa (1850), James Prior (1851), Sarah Jane (1854), Frederick William (1856) and Jemima Annie (1858), all named after members of their mother's family.

Although born in rural Leicestershire, James Kirk senior was a milliner and manufacturer of straw hats, with shops in the city centre at Peck Lane, Hounds Gate and Pelham Street. Later, as fashions changed, the business declined and downsized to premises at 20 South Parade. Both the Kirks and the Priors were Methodists and part of a large community of Dissenters in the city. From his father James Prior inherited his faith, his deep sense of morality, a love of the countryside and of reading. He told Fisher *'From my father I got my love of reading and walking, and probably writing, for he had a gravely exact way of expressing himself with his pen'.*[ii] However, reading matter was strictly censored by Mr Kirk, and it was not until his late teens that Prior encountered Dickens, Shakespeare and Sir Walter Scott. The impression was clearly explosive and Prior would continue to draw inspiration from these writers throughout his own writing career.

School was first a small preparatory school run by the Misses Goodall, then ten years at a school run by Mr. Porter. Fisher reports: *'I have it from one of his schoolfellows, he was brilliant. He himself says he was desultory and indolent. Of slight physique, he was yet very active, given to field sports and to long rambles in the country.'* Certainly, Prior enjoyed long walks in the countryside, often gathering material for his books, well into later life.

Prior appears to have been close to his siblings. In his manuscript collection of poems, now in the Nottinghamshire County Archives, and in the small selection published by Fisher in 1925,[iii] there is a poem dedicated to his younger sister, Jemima, known as Jennie:

To Jennie (9th May 1889)

Dearest my sister, if I'd half-a-crown,
I'd buy a Thackery or flower glass,
A picture or a shepherdess in brass,
That so my kindly memory might be shown

Of what I owe you. But I'm told a poet,
If he be short of cash and eke of credit,
Puts down a rhyme for every penny in debit,
And so discharges much as he doth owe it.

If rhymes would serve, I'd call up every noun
That lies a maid yet in the barren lap
Of Walker's Dictionary, if by hap
Such be as have not donned the wedding gown.

And each to some fresh-blooming adjective,
Hay-scented of the happy golden time,
When reason meant one thing, another rhyme,
Or to some younker attribute I'd wive;

And find substantial predicates each bride
To give away with formal heavy hand,
And call for bridesmaids round, in smiling band,
The prettiest adverbs of the countryside.

This would I do, if doing 'twould behoove
To stop the large claim of my creditor
With something on account, though little; or
If rhyming will not serve, I'll pay with love.

When his younger brother Frederick William died in 1899, Prior again turned to verse:

In Memoriam, FWK (1899)

The ship sails forth into infinite ocean,
We stand, we watch her go,
Or fast or slow,

As distance guesses darkly of her motion;

Until passivity seems to have bound
The inevitable push
In solemn hush.
Yet sinks the hull behind the watery round.

Now at the point of heaven and earth's division
The mast's sky-pointing finger
Awhile doth linger;
Then that too passes wholly from our vision.
Call her not back, delay her not one minute.
That gathered merchandise,
The gold, corn, spice –
Except she sail, there is no profit in it.

Waft an adieu; agree that all is well.
Did ye not stand and see
How prosperously
The breath of heaven was quickening her sail.

Mr Kirk was clearly ambitious for his eldest son and so James Prior was articled to a Nottingham Solicitor, Mr Rothera (the firm of Rotheras still exists) with the intention that he should become a lawyer. James Prior, however, did not take to the law and *'instead of devoting his time to the study of law, he gave most of his time to the study of languages and literature, especially Greek, and the Greek classics were a delight to him throughout his life.'*[iv]

After three years, he was not at all ready for his final examinations. There was a confrontation with his father, but James Prior stood firm in his determination to become a writer. It may be a result of this bitter clash that he wrote as James Prior rather than James Kirk. Success was elusive and at the age of 27 he took up a teaching post at a boy's boarding school in Southport. After only one term he moved to another school in Merton, Surrey and began to study for a degree with London University. Prior failed to complete these studies and did not take his degree because he developed a serious eye condition which rendered him almost blind. We have no information about the precise nature of this complaint, but it continued to recur periodically throughout his life and caused him great discomfort.

In 1880 his father died and for a while Prior tried to help his sisters run the business. The women of the family had long been involved in the business and clearly had a better feel for it, two of them taking over after a year, but he remained partly involved until it folded completely in 1914. During this time Prior began to help an uncle, William Kirk, who was a butcher and grazier living in Uppingham, Rutland. His business was in difficulties and Prior invested money to help, losing much of it. This uncle had grazing interests in the area around Blidworth, Notts, and James was frequently in the area to check on affairs. Here he developed a great love for the countryside and the people of the area, particularly the rhythms of their speech and this was to become a major feature of his subsequent writing. So, although this period did nothing for Prior's finances, it provided him with material which would emerge in his most successful novel, *Forest Folk*. During this period of five years he also fell in love with a cousin, Lily, fifteen years his junior, and they married in 1886.

Prior produced some early works during this time and succeeded in getting them published – *'Three Shots from a Popgun – a tale'* in 1880 published by Remington & Co., London, a verse play set in 14th century Spain *Don Pedro The Cruel* in 1882 published by Hamilton, Adams & Co., London & Nottingham, and two further plays, *John Smith of London* and *Live and Let Live,* published as one volume in 1883 – but this was hardly the literary success he craved.

JAMES AND LILY – A LOVE MATCH

In his manuscript collection of poems[v], there are some sweet love poems dated 3rd April 1886, not the loftiest verse, but an indication of Prior's feelings:

'I love you', written down and spoken out,
And softly whispered to my listening heart,
The sweetest vocables to either part
Of hearing or of seeing; beyond doubt
Received by one who'd lost the happy art
Of hearing rain fall in a time of drought;
Intensified and underlined by her who'd scorn
The talk of wounds unless she felt the smart.

A month later, on 12th May, Lily accepted Prior's proposal of marriage and he wrote as only a besotted lover can:

Sweet Lily,
Accept this silly
Betrothal gift from thy fond lover,
In token
Of what cannot be spoken,
Within the limits of a mortal cover;

Bought not with money,
Dearest one,
Night by night I've waked
To steal a little honey,
Not of Helicon,
Where the muses show their beauty naked
But from the humble bees
Of our own leas;

A thing of little pride,
Put in a vessel mean and rough,
To make enough
I'll add the total of my love beside.

The couple briefly returned to Nottingham, then for three years rented rooms in Radcliffe on Trent in a house on Bingham Road opposite the turning to Lorne Grove. They were clearly deeply in love, but most importantly, Lily believed in Prior's writing. She encouraged him to concentrate on his art rather than forcing himself into a business life that he hated. He still had a little independent money and she was a good manager, so although they would never be rich, Prior was free to pursue his dreams with Lily at his side.

Lily gave birth to two daughters, Margaret in 1889 and then Dorothy in 1890, so the rooms in Radcliffe must have been crowded and noisy, not ideal for a writer to produce good work. Shortly after the Census return of 1891, Prior, Lily and their daughters moved to Bingham, renting Brusty Cottage on Fisher Lane. This is now No. 19 and was re-named Lushai Cottage in the 1940s by the then owner, Col. Johnson, who had served in the Indian Army and named his cottage for a range of hills in north-east India.

MR KIRK OF BINGHAM

Brusty Cottage was a pretty 18th century cottage with two rooms downstairs on either side of the front door, two bedrooms upstairs, a kitchen-scullery at the back, a cellar which pre-dated the rest of the house, an outside privy and a well for water in the garden. The rooms were quite small, but this was a home for the Kirks, and it clearly suited Prior's temperament. There was a strong Methodist community in Bingham, and most significantly, it was only a brisk walk away from the banks of the River Trent.

Brusty, now Lushai Cottage today

A son, Walter, was born at Brusty Cottage on 11th July 1892. Prior was also busy producing two novels which really showed his developing talent: *Renie* published by Hutchinson in 1895 and *Ripple and Flood* published in London by Hutchinson in 1897 with a simultaneous release in Philadelphia.

Renie is a sad tale of a girl who discovers that her 'mother' is in fact a foster mother, and goes in search of her natural father, who turns out to be a popular – if clearly hypocritical – preacher. It starts in Bingham, which Prior calls Bawton, then continues into Nottingham. The opening scenes describe a children's May Day pageant organised by the Bawton Band of Hope, a Temperance Society, in the Primitive Methodist Chapel. Similar children's festivals are described in Adelaide Wortley's 1954 *History of Bingham*, and I have no doubt that Prior drew on what he saw and experienced in Bingham.[vi] The Methodist and Primitive Methodist chapels were only a stone's throw from Brusty Cottage, and he must have attended one or other of them frequently.

Once the action moved into Nottingham, he could draw on his early experience of the city. In an article for *The Nottinghamshire Countryside* magazine in 1941, Ivory Buchan wrote of *Renie*: '*It is melodramatic and wooden and the style is unsure, but it has hints of promise ... there are some clever character sketches ... and there is a description of a Nottingham slum which shows not merely an observant eye and a feeling for locale but also a certain social consciousness and sympathy with poor people.*'

In 1990 James Best wrote an article for the *Sneinton Magazine* tracing some of the locations in *Renie's* story and praising Prior's depictions of places which he clearly knew well, concluding "*We are unlikely to find a more vivid description of one of Nottingham's less fashionable quarters in the 1880s.*"[vii] Throughout his writing Prior would show a keen eye for the details of the living conditions of the poor and a sympathy for their struggles.

Stephen Fisher wrote of *Renie*: '*it is not to be compared with his later achievements. With* Ripple and Flood *he rose at last to the full dignity of his art,'* and I have to agree. However, *Renie* does lay the foundations for Prior's best work with its local colour and use of dialect.

Ripple and Flood is set in the Trent Valley and looking at old maps it is possible to trace the route Prior would have taken on his walks to the villages of Hoveringham and Caythorpe where most of the action takes place. From Fisher Lane, Prior would cross the Market Square, turn up Station Street and take the bridge across the Grantham to Nottingham railway line, then follow footpaths which are still there today towards East Bridgford and Kneeton, where a steep track leads down to the river. In Prior's time there was a ferry here which took foot passengers across to Hoveringham. It was no more than a man and a rowing boat; weightier traffic would need to go upstream to Gunthorpe where there was a chain ferry and later a new iron toll bridge, opened in 1875. The Hoveringham ferry became a major feature of the new book – the female lead, Ivy Sivil, is the daughter of the ferryman. The jetty can still be seen today; the ferryman's cottage is a private house, and the site of the old boat house is a tangle of brambles beside the gate through to the walk along the river. Walking through the village of Caythorpe with a copy of the book in one's hand feels like walking into a movie of the novel, so much remains as it was in Prior's day. Prior's intimate knowledge of this part of the Trent Valley was poured into his writing to create a vivid picture of the river and its banks from its mildest to its most turbulent moods.

In *Ripple and Flood* Prior once again changes the names of the villages – Caythorpe becomes Cockerby, Hoveringham is Elham, and Lowdham with its station becomes Clayton. The story is told through the eyes of a boy, Edward Allius, growing up in his uncle's house, gradually coming to understand the tragedy of his own parent's history.

Young Edward is destined to become a painter and even as a child he has a heightened appreciation of the colours of river and bank: *'My prime consolation was neither book nor friend but what entered by my eye...the miracle of colours on a spink's back ... the surface of the river dappled with light and shade ... a low marly cliff, red streaked with white, crowned with flickering green under which the river is dark and still'.*

One of Prior's most enduring characters is Ivy Sivil, the ferryman's daughter. She is orphaned when the Trent in flood sweeps her parents away. Like a feral cat, she runs away from the dreaded Workhouse at Southwell, burns the hated workhouse dress and lives wild wearing Edward's spare set of boy's clothes. She speaks in the broadest of Nottinghamshire dialect. Later, she blossoms into the respected and charismatic Salvation Army preacher, Sister Ruth, and her speech is modified by the influence of the Bible. This time there is a happier ending but not before past sins of addiction, anger and jealousy are faced up to and atoned for. This idea of repentance and forgiveness was to be a recurring motif in Prior's work.

These two books were almost certainly written at Brusty Cottage and reflect Prior's growing affection for Bingham and its surrounding countryside. In one of the later scenes in *Ripple and Flood*, Edward goes to see Sister Ruth preach. The crowds are almost suffocating, and he struggles to get a place from which to see her. Prior appears to have taken this scene from a report of the opening of the first Primitive Methodist Chapel in Bingham in 1818 (over the current Horse and Plough pub) when huge crowds turned up to hear an American guest preacher and a popular woman preacher.[viii] It also marked his maturity as a writer; Stephen Fisher commented that it *'is the most intensely powerful thing Mr Prior has done'.*[ix]

The ferry at Hoveringham c1900, and below, as it looks today

Ripple and Flood received some favourable reviews. *The Saturday Review:*

> 'An excellent piece of work, sober and restrained, but powerful throughout.'

The Times:

> 'Ripple and Flood is a story with an atmosphere of great freshness, and with descriptions of country life and scenery that reminds us of Mr. Thomas Hardy. A story, indeed, which it would be unfair to describe as merely creditable; the two brothers are both striking characters, while Ivy Sivil is almost as attractive as a Salvation lassie as in boy's clothes.'

The Scotsman:

> 'Vivid, impressive, and original, the story rivets the attention right to the last line, and the book is laid down with a feeling of admiration for the author's glowing imagination and his skill in reproducing its conjurings. Altogether it is a book which deserves a hearty reception from the public.'[x]

While *The Times* reviewer compared Prior to Thomas Hardy, *'The Literary Lounger'* in *The Sketch* cast him as the heir to Dickens:

> 'The hero in his boyhood would be a real Dickens' character, if he were only a trifle more genial; and in the scene where the meek murderer crawls in from the rainy night, "with some sort of motion, not a human walk, leaving a slimy trail on the floor like a snail," Mr Prior shows the same power of haunting horror as Dickens used to exercise. The master who made the 'Marchioness', too, would not have disdained the creation of Ivy.'

Ripple and Flood was also published in the USA by J. B. Lippincott & Co., the largest and best known publisher at the time. How the American audience received the Nottinghamshire dialect of Ivy and her fellows is only to be guessed at.

Prior must have been encouraged by the success of *Ripple and Flood*; with a growing family, and congenial surroundings, he was at last able to realise his literary ambitions.

At some point between 1897 and 1900 the Kirk family were forced to move again. Brusty Cottage was sold, and by 1900 a new owner had moved in. Just around the corner on The Banks, two pairs of new cottages had been built in 1896 by a local developer, James Walker. These were still modest dwellings with only two rooms on each floor, but the rooms were a little bigger, with taller ceilings and a brighter feel. There was a pump, rather than a well, and a washhouse and privy in the spacious garden. There was probably gas light in the house and a gas streetlight just outside. The Kirks moved into one of the pair called Banks Cottages, today No.22 The Banks, (houses in Bingham were not given street numbers until the 1940s).

The Banks was an area of orchards. Bingham was famous for apples and plums, including the Victoria Plum which was supposedly bred in Bingham. Banks Cottages and neighbouring Grove Cottages were part of a gradual but relentless development. The Kirks looked out onto a dirt road with orchards beyond – a small remnant of which can still be seen opposite the cemetery at the eastern end of The Banks.

It seems likely that this move came after the publication of *Ripple and Flood*, and once settled, Prior began work on what would become his most successful book, *Forest Folk.*

The Banks 1909 – the Kirk family lived in the second pair of cottages, on the left, where the streetlight is. I like to think that Prior might have been sitting in the front room, writing, when this picture was taken.

22 The Banks today

FOREST FOLK

Forest Folk was published by Heinemann in May 1901. In his 1925 pamphlet about James Prior, Stephen Fisher wrote:

> *'Some of the qualities of "Forest Folk" were so plain as to be undeniable. The dramatic force, the racy humour, the virility, the fidelity, these were instantly admitted. What was less obtrusive, the easy mastery of language, the balance of characterisation, the tenderness, the spiritual delicacy, the poetic sense of landscape and atmosphere, these were only hinted at by an occasional reviewer. One went so far as to say: "That which Blackmore has done for the Devonshire Moors, that which Thomas Hardy has done for the vales of Wessex, that surely shall James Prior accomplish for Nottinghamshire." A safe prophecy, seeing that it was already practically fulfilled.'*

In spite of such a confident assessment by this anonymous reviewer, Prior's success was modest, but *Forest Folk* remains his most famous book. The influence of Sir Walter Scott can be seen in his choice of a broad historical background – the Napoleonic Wars and the Luddite disturbances – against which he weaves his story. The action is set in the countryside around Blidworth in the early years of the 19th century. Drive down the lane at Blidworth Bottoms today and you are still surrounded by the fields and hedgerows that Arthur Skrene notices as he arrives on horseback to look over his new inheritance, High Farm. Here he first encounters Nell Rideout, dressed in men's clothes and supervising the ploughing of her fields with only her wild, red hair escaping from her hat to indicate who she really is. The Skrenes and the Rideouts clash over locked gates – a reference to the controversial Enclosure Acts – farming methods and local justice but the growing attraction between Arthur and Nell is obvious. Dr Tony Shaw has written at length about Nell as a representation of 'The New Woman'[xi]; she defies gender stereotypes, class prejudices and drives the action forward with a verve that makes her thoroughly modern. Even the character of Lois Skrene, Arthur's sister, who appears meek and mild at first, shows her mettle by defying her brother to defend Nell's handsome brother Tant in court and then hides him in Arthur's house when he falls foul of the law again. Arthur and Tant both learn from their contact with strong women and become better versions of themselves as a consequence.

As in *Ripple and Flood*, Prior's intimate knowledge of and love for the countryside through every season abounds in *Forest Folk*. Jean Anabel Cooper wrote in her 1965 article for the *Nottinghamshire Countryside* magazine, that he:

> *'described the grey, desolate wastes of gorse and ling in the cold wet weather of mid-November so vividly as to make the reader almost feel the drip of water from overhead branches, the driving rain, soaking mist and wet sticky clay underfoot.'*

There is humour, some salutary lessons about the evils of alcohol, breath-taking rides across the countryside, violence and skulduggery, incitement and betrayal, and a happy ending for only one of the couples. But above all, *Forest Folk* captures the language of the common people, the field workers, weavers and miners who lived in the Nottinghamshire countryside. The lower orders speak in the broadest of Nottinghamshire dialect while the Skrenes, southerners and gentry, speak Standard English. The Rideouts, Nell and Tant, are socially halfway between the two, and can modify their use of the dialect when it suits them, to move between social classes. Reading this dialect for the first time can feel confusing and even hard work, but the trick is to read aloud and let your 'ear' and 'eye' get attuned.

Forest Folk is the only one of Prior's books currently available in a modern edition. Thanks to the revival of interest in local authors, *Forest Folk* was re-published by Leen Editions and Spokesman Books, Nottingham, in 2017. In the Foreword, Rowena Edlin-White writes:

> *'The plot has all the ingredients of a rollicking historical adventure, but Prior transcends the merely sensational by two supreme gifts: his sense of place and his ear for dialect.'*

If Thomas Hardy sometimes used the vernacular of Wessex in his novels, Prior went a step further and made Nottinghamshire dialect central to his work. In *Renie, Ripple and Flood* and *Forest Folk*, characters speak on the page just as Prior heard them speak in the villages he had come to know so well. A friend of mine suggested that since Prior's eyesight was so often impaired, his sense of hearing became heightened – an interesting thought – but whatever the reason, Prior was closely attuned to dialect. This can be a barrier at first to a modern reader but Prior manages to pull us along, even if some of the expressions feel foreign, by the force of his narrative.

Subsequent editions of *Forest Folk*, such as the Nelson pocket edition of 1918, included a glossary to help readers through the more obscure words and phrases. He continued to be committed to using the colour, rhythms and cadences of local dialect through his later novels, and the collection and recording of the dialect of Nottinghamshire became a major aspect of his life's work.

Contemporary reviews of *Forest Folk* were positive and sometimes enthusiastic. *The Athenæum:*

> *'The book reminds us of George Eliot in the unforced and racy style in which bucolic characters from farmer to day-man speak from its pages, and the way in which these characters are set in their natural surroundings. It is, perhaps, in the female characters that the author is most successful, so much so, that we have found ourselves wondering at times if the name on the title-page is not a woman's disguise. Man or woman, the author is to be congratulated on a really clever novel.'*

The Daily Telegraph:

> *'Mr. James Prior develops his characters and portrays their individualities in the course of his story successfully, and his pages are full of the dialect and the scenery of their environment.'*

Illustrated London News:

> *'It is seldom that in a story told with so much delicacy and restraint, we find chapters of such virile force and fun as 'With Mr. Pepper's Hounds,' and the series describing Tant Rideout's midnight visits to Ben Foat and his wife Deb. In these last, and constantly throughout the story, Mr. Prior takes risks, but he always bears himself safely through. In a word, he has produced a book of quite unusual quality, and we very heartily congratulate him on his achievement.'*

Publishers' Circular:

> *'Readers with a taste for the study of rural character must obtain the book for themselves, and we can promise them hearty enjoyment in its perusal.'*

I think Prior might have chuckled at being mistaken for a woman on the one hand, and praised as 'virile' on the other! Heinemann must have eagerly anticipated Prior's next book.

EBB AND FLOW

Forest Folk was a success, but as so many authors find out, the follow up book is make or break. Sadly, Prior's next book, *Hyssop,* (June 1904) was a flop. Widely considered to be his weakest work, it was not a success with the public and didn't sell well, and I can see why. The story is set in another Trentside village, Burton Joyce, which Prior calls Crifton, and opens with Eva, a casualty from a train crash at the level crossing, suffering from total amnesia, being taken in by the Sample family. *The Times* commented:

> *'What will live in the memory is the picture of the quiet home life of a family in the tradesman class ... very clever it is ... Eva in her state of forgetfulness, a grown woman with the 'innocence and charm of a child', is a thing of beauty.'*

The Sample family consists of a widow and four adult siblings, and their affectionate banter may reflect some of Prior's own childhood memories. The eldest brother, Ira, works at a draper's shop in Nottingham but is privately studying to become a doctor; Jim is a teacher with ambitions to become a clergyman, and is an incurable romantic. Both fall in love with their pretty, mysterious guest, inevitably causing tension between them. The sisters are typical of Prior's strong-minded women: Vinnie is a 'typewriter' but wants to be a journalist and is already writing local articles for the Nottingham newspaper, while the more serious Silla works in a bookshop and has a secret ambition to become a factory inspector.

Eva turns out to be less charming and innocent than she seems; as her memory returns it transpires that she has been dragged into a life of vice by addiction to gin.

The book lacks the strong sense of place that both *Ripple and Flood* and *Forest Folk* had, and the characters are 'thin' when compared to Edward and Ivy or Nell and Arthur. The plot lacks development: the only excitement comes when Eva runs out of her wedding to Jim and flees to London, but even then Prior seems to run out of steam and leaves us to guess at what happens next. In the end Eva is 'saved' from degradation not through marriage to either Jim or Ira, but through friendship with another working-class woman, a pleasing and unexpectedly feminist twist. However, the colour and vivacity of language which came with his previous use of dialect is missing and the writing feels overly formal, rather stuffy and old-fashioned. After this failure Heinemann dropped Prior and his career effectively stalled, and that was a shame because his last two published books were possibly his best work.

The last two of Prior's published works were *A Walking Gentleman*, published in August 1907 by Constable, and *Fortuna Chance,* also published by Constable in 1910. Both of these have very modern themes, the first describing a journey of self-discovery and the second featuring a single mother bringing up her son in spite of social disapproval.

A Walking Gentleman is a journey of self-discovery. Lord Beiley is rich, aristocratic, privileged, and thoroughly bored with life. On the eve of his wedding to Lady Sally – rich, clever and beautiful – he goes for a walk to get away from all the fuss of wedding preparations. He intends to just go to the end of the drive, but he carries on, encounters a cartload of working men and women off for a day's jaunt, joins them and never turns back. When he realises that he has missed his wedding he is too embarrassed to return so walks on and on. In the next weeks and months, he mixes with people whose social rank is as far below him as possible, but each teaches him something about the value of life. He spends half a day as a stone breaker, meets an innocent child whose simple wisdom enchants him, mixes with rogues and vagrants, a dissolute money lender and his rapacious daughter, ends up in prison, falls into a burning peat bog, and even contemplates ending his life. At one point he finds himself at a seaside resort on the Lincolnshire coast where he joins up with a seasonal entertainer in a 'blackface' act singing minstrel songs for a few pence. Finally, returning to the countryside near to Lady Sally's estate, he finds work and peace with a farmer who is also a lay preacher, a humane and considerate employer who gives him shelter and doesn't pry too deeply into what is clearly an unusual and painful past.

Lady Sally is another of Prior's impressive women. She is rarely in the centre of the action but her presence is like a hovering guardian angel. When Beiley jilts her, her family and friends are furious, initiating a manhunt to drag him back and commit him to an asylum – for how could any sane man run out on such an advantageous marriage? Lady Sally resists this, intuiting that there are demons which Beiley has to chase down in his own time. Once the initial hue and cry subsides, Lady Sally follows him from a distance, just making sure that he is still alive and waiting for the right moment to welcome him back. She tracks him to the coast where there is an edgy meeting between them, both pretending not to recognise the other, but Beiley hides behind his blackface disguise and is not yet ready to face her. Eventually she provides the final nudge which brings him back to her, a penitent who expects to be cast out, ready to beg forgiveness before emigrating to the Americas to start a new life. In this last encounter Sally has the upper hand; Beiley's fate is her's to decide. He is now a very different man, a better man who understands her value and how much he still has to learn, and this is the husband that Sally wants for herself.

In this book Prior again gives us vibrant descriptions of the countryside from Nottingham, through the villages to Retford, Gainsborough and across Lincolnshire to the coast, then back to the boggy Nottinghamshire 'carrs'. He gives the locations different names, but anyone familiar with the East Midlands can recognise where Beiley wanders easily enough. His characters cover the whole gamut of society, from aristocrat to vagrant, saint to sinner. Dialect is again used to great effect and there are passages of almost slapstick humour reminiscent of the 'rude mechanicals' of Shakespeare's *A Midsummer's Night Dream*.

Many people think *A Walking Gentleman* is Prior's best book. Stephen Fisher loved it, writing:

'It is full of movement, of character, of humour robust and subtle, of the poetic sense, of spirituality ... To me it is a piece of virile yet delicate realism; it is what I imagine its author intended it to be, "a procession of life of extraordinary richness and variety." ... It is a subtle theme worked out with infinite subtlety.'

It certainly strikes chords with today's preoccupation with 'finding oneself' through learning from others.

The Daily Mail reviewed *A Walking Gentleman* favourably:

'No one knows better than a reviewer, who reads all sorts of novels, how good is Mr. Prior's book. Here is a real piece of work; here is an author who can portray scenes and draw characters faithfully and without exaggeration, a writer who thinks and is not afraid to give his thoughts...Mr. Prior's work is stamped with a sincerity which we too rarely find in a novel, although no novel is of any worth without it.'

The Manchester Guardian:

'The Book will take hold of you by its vitality, its good temper, and its mellow humour.'

21

and *The Athenaeum* optimistically predicted:

"The book will dwell in the memory when most novels have faded from it."

Prior's last published novel was *Fortuna Chance*, (Constable & Co., 1910). In this he returned to a broad historical theme, this time the Jacobite Rising of 1745 led by Charles Edward Stuart, 'Bonnie Prince Charlie', against the Hanoverian King George II. Fortuna Chance is a society lady who finds herself pregnant after an affair and dubious 'marriage' with a social inferior who then deserts her. Defying convention and social pressure, she decides to raise her son, Roland, on her own. Prior describes her as *'one of the first of that new thing in the modern world, an emancipated woman.'* When detractors pun her name as 'Mis-chance', she changes her son's name to 'Surety', also a pun on his father's name 'Bond', and settles in a cottage in Sherwood Forest, near the Byron estate at Newstead. Fortuna and her son are Catholics and supporters of the old Stuart kings, so when Bonnie Prince Charlie arrives with his Highlander forces, Roland is keen to join them. A series of mishaps means that he misses them at Derby (the furthest extent of the invasion) but is instead arrested for a murder of which he is altogether innocent. The nearest he gets to the Prince's army is an encounter with a group of renegade Highlander deserters who are doing a bit of private enterprise looting and pillaging on their way home.

Prior uses his local knowledge to give us vivid scenes of forest life and a range of minor local characters in the manner of *Forest Folk*. These include some real local figures, in particular the 5th Lord Byron and his cousin and neighbour Sir William Chaworth.[xii] However, it is the common folk who buzz with vitality, speak in the dialect of the area, and give us a cross section of local life.

One of the early themes in the book is the growth of Methodism and the sectarian hatreds of the day. Fortuna and Roland are of course seen as dubious outsiders because of their Catholicism. The Jacobites saw the Hanoverian kings as Protestant imposters who should be deposed, so anti-Catholic sentiment was at a high point in the period, and Catholic Emancipation did not come until 1829. Dissent from the Protestant side was also viewed with suspicion. This was the period when John Wesley's Methodism was beginning to spread in the East Midlands. Prior gives us a striking picture of an intrepid preacher coming into the district to win the common people over to the Bible and temperance. He is met with hostility and violence from both the authorities and the regulars at the local alehouse.

As in *Forest Folk*, Prior uses his local knowledge to describe Roland's journey across the county and into the Derbyshire peaks. With his intimate knowledge of landscape, flora and fauna and the effects of weather and light, he takes us on breathless gallops through forest, moor and cliff as Roland flees from his pursuers. There can be no doubt that Prior walked these hills himself as he researched this book. There is love interest in the person of Alfa, a gypsy girl, who helps Roland, and who bears a passing resemblance in looks and character to Ivy Sivil. There are some wonderful minor characters. I particularly like the two indomitable Derbyshire sisters who take Roland in and nurse him when he is injured and who bicker affectionately like characters in Mrs. Gaskell's *Cranford*. They turn out to be fellow Jacobites and, unbeknown to Roland, cousins of his mother Fortuna. In a discussion about Fortuna's ill-fated affair, Mistress Ann expresses the constraints facing women just as strongly as Charlotte Bronte's Jane Eyre[xiii], saying:

'The man either fights or excuses himself, whichever is the easier ... The woman can neither fight nor excuse herself, she must sit mum, a target for every roving shot.'

In the end Roland is saved from the hangman's noose by the courageous and quick-witted actions of the women in his life, Fortuna is reconciled with her family, and Roland's father faces up to his responsibilities. All in all, a very satisfactory ending.

Fortuna Chance has all the elements of Prior's best writing. The descriptions of the Derbyshire High Peak in winter are chillingly bleak, his minor characters have energy and local colour, there is jeopardy at every turn and there is a final courtroom confrontation and unmasking of Roland's father, worthy of a Hollywood thriller. Reviewers liked it.

The Times:

'A good tale, given with great fulness and fertility of interest.'

The Scotsman:

'There is a wealth of local scenery and customs, strong situations and moving passions in the romance.'

The Westminster Gazette:

> *'It was a clever conception of the '45, and it is handled in a way that warms the heart… 'Fortuna Chance' is, by a long way, the best tale he has written.'*

Whatever literary influences others might have seen in his books, Prior himself always maintained that his work came solely from his own imagination. During a period of just fifteen years he produced six novels, four of which – *Ripple and Flood, Forest Folk, A Walking Gentleman* and *Fortuna Chance*, surely deserve to rank as 'classics'. I would argue that this achievement was largely down to the happiness and stability which Lily created for Prior in their Bingham home.

FAMILY LIFE AT BANKS COTTAGE

My initial interest in Prior was as a writer who had lived in Bingham, my own hometown for over forty years. As well as reading his books, I wanted to understand what he was like as a person, so I looked for any sources which could throw light on his personality and family life during this most productive period of his life.

What was Prior like? There are a few reports that cast light on his nature. Stephen Fisher records:

> 'To watch the growth of one of Mr Prior's books is a curious and valuable experience. He is very deliberate. Many things arising out of the exigencies of his life will conspire to thwart and delay him. He waits, serenely, on opportunity. His hours of actual writing are of necessity few, but his hours of thoughtful preparation are many. His themes are expansive, and in the course of their development gain much from the passing experiences of his life. He will go for a ramble and bring home a new character, a quaint saying, a fine atmospheric effect, a striking landscape. He is conscientious in small things: he will search and question diligently about a mere detail. He will travel miles afoot to verify his local colour. He refuses to be hurried. If his theme baffles him a while, he lays it aside until there comes to him one of his favourite nights, a radiant night with soft clouds drifting across the path of the moon. Into such a night he will take his difficulty and return triumphant'.[xiv]

Certainly, the novels show that Prior knew the countryside he described from personal experience. He took on average three years to bring a new book to publication and had time to do thorough research especially when he used an historical setting. To explore the towns and villages of the Trent Valley and the East Midlands, he could have used not just the footpaths but also the railway lines that criss-crossed the region before the cuts of the 'Beeching Axe' reduced them to the few we see today. Railways often appear in his novels and I get the feeling that he enjoyed travelling by train.

Prior was a loving father. In his poetry manuscript there are a couple of ditties that he wrote for the infant Margaret:

Margaret's Evening Prayer (1ˢᵗ June 1891)

Here I am,
God's little lamb.
Soon the light
Will go away; {or Now the light has gone away}
God made night
Before the day.
God made me
And Dorothy.

God's lambkins rest
Safe in nest.
Dear God, kiss me
On the cheek.
It will bless me
In my sleep,
Happy make
When I awake
Amen

In April 1905 Prior wrote for Margaret's album:

A little song to fill a little page,
As brief as is a sparrow's roundelay
To his brown partner listening in the hedge;
Whose last is to his first as yes to yea;
A little song to fill a little page.

A little song to fill a little page,
As simple as the gaze of children's eyes,
Through whose clear blue shines trust without a pledge,
Love without passion, joy without surprise;
A little song to fill a little page.

When *Hyssop* was published Prior, gave a copy to his younger daughter, Dorothy, as a belated birthday gift with this inscription on the flyleaf:

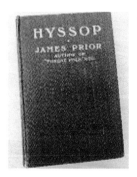
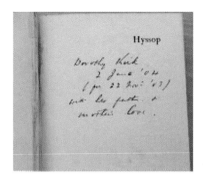

*"Dorothy Kirk 2 June '04 (for 22 Nov '03)
with her father & mother's love"*

The Census of 1911 shows that a second son was born to Lily and James in 1908, christened Harold. The older children, Margaret, Dorothy and Walter, almost certainly attended the Wesleyan School on Kirk Hill, built in 1850. This was a rival to the Church of England School near the parish church, built by Canon Robert Miles, and must have been very popular because it was extended, nearly doubling in size, in 1860. It continued in use until the new County School was built on School Lane in 1909 for juniors and infants. Harold in his turn, probably attended the new school on School Lane, now the Robert Miles Infants School. The Wesleyan school is two private residences today.

The old Wesleyan School on Kirkhill, Bingham

Prior had published some short plays in his early years, and it seems he continued to write dramas. In his collection of poems *Canticles,* he included an extract from a verse play, *The King's Wards,* which may have been intended either for the school or for a Sunday School performance.

The Kirks were Methodists and James regularly attended the Wesleyan Chapel on Union Street with Lily and the children.[xv] There was also a Primitive Chapel and Temperance Hall off Long Acre, which would have been just a step away from both the Kirk homes. Temperance, and the evil effects of drink, feature prominently in most of the books. Religion is portrayed as an improving influence but Prior was not narrow minded about denomination. He clearly favoured low church, dissenting sects but could acknowledge the beneficial effects of attending Anglican services. Amongst his characters there are worldly and philandering curates, well-meaning clergymen, a domineering Salvationist Captain, sincere and humane lay preachers, devoted worshippers, and even sincere Catholics. It seems that Prior approved of faith, especially when it guided action. What he disapproved of was sectarian hatred.

The old Wesleyan Chapel, Union Street,
now rebuilt as a modern Methodist centre

The former Independent Methodist (Primitive) Chapel and Temperance Hall off Long Acre; both Anglicans and Methodists supported the temperance movement. Prior lived a stone's throw from here.

In 1911 the family was reduced by emigration. Walter, aged 19, took advantage of a scheme promoted by the Canadian Government to attract labour to its emptier provinces. Young, fit men were offered land if they would make the journey across the Atlantic and settle in Manitoba as farmers. Walter was not the only Bingham lad to take up this scheme. His turn came in 1911, a few weeks before the Census. Walter sailed from Liverpool to St. John's, New Brunswick on board the *Virginian* in March 1911. He settled in Beausejour, Manitoba, 46 km north of Winnipeg.[xvi]

It seems possible that Prior accompanied his son to Liverpool to see him off. This must have been an emotional parting since it was unlikely that Walter would ever return. Three weeks later Prior appears on the Census record staying about 40 kilometres away in the Welsh town of Ruthin as a visitor at a temperance hotel. What was he doing there? Perhaps he was researching a new novel – we just don't know.

Meanwhile, Lily was also visiting but this time in Harpenden, near St. Albans in Hertfordshire. Back at Banks Cottage, Margaret, now 21, was a 'student for the teaching profession', Dorothy and Harold were at home and Edith Mary Kirk (widow) – presumably a relative – was there as housekeeper.

In the following years Lily became ill, and she died aged only 48 on 9th March 1914. Prior was obviously devastated. He wrote three poems which give us some idea of his profound feelings:

In Memoriam 9ᵗʰ March 1914

1

I have eaten my fill,
Have laughed and have wept,
Have loved and been loved,
Have humoured my will,
And held it reproved,
Said my say and forbore,
Have waked and have slept;
Now I sleep and shall wake no more.

Still not your tread
About my feet,
Hush not your speech
 Above my head
To a whisper pitch,
Stay not your hand on the door.
I do you to weet,
That I sleep and shall wake no more.

2

Girl and woman,
I have lived soberly, kindly, religiously,
Labouring beyond my sufficiency of strength,
Cheerfully giving out of a scanty store,
Solacing myself with unpurchasable pleasures,
Sweet simplicities.

Dear was my voice to song
And mine eyes to laughter,
Though often wrested by the compulsion
Of sorrow.
I have devised no deceit,
Imagined no malice,
Dealt neither in two-faced phrases
Nor crafty caresses.
Hear then the dumbness of my wan lips;
Crown me with praise,
Cover me with flowers.

Friend and matron,
I have fulfilled all the functions of my being;
Have yielded my neck to the yoke of fellowship,
Have sung to some and some have sung to me,
Have been taken by a lover into his arms,
By a man into his life.
I hid a secret in my heart,
A babe under my heart;
I was that only consummate thing,
A mother.

Lo, I have given suck,
Counsel and comfort.
I leave no division of money
But legacies of love.
Heed then the appeal of my shut eyes,
Crown me with praise,
Cover me with flowers.

3
Thou art ever with me
And all I have is thine,
The head, the hand, the touch of fellowship,
The laugh, if laughter yet will come at call,
The tear, if tear a dry grief can let fall,
Whether the rags of failure sit on me,
Or wintry flowers of late success enwreathe me,
Yea, thine is all.
The joy I quaff, the woe I sip,
The accident, the dream, the deep design,
The hope above me and the fear beneath me,
Even all and more is thine.

And thou art ever with me,
Though I be here and thou be gone;
Though from thy face or voice arrive no sign
To the gross organs of my strained endeavour,
The hand from hand untravelled mystery sever;
Yea, with me ever.
Nothing can disannul what hath been done.

Whether life fill my lungs or death unbreathe me,
Thou art ever with me,
And all I have is thine.

I find these poems deeply touching and indicative of a sincere love for a much younger woman who must have taken quite a leap of faith to marry an impecunious, aspiring writer. In the first two poems Prior gives Lily a voice from beyond the grave and expresses all his respect and admiration for her character. There is perhaps a reference here to the Greek classics that Prior so loved, with the spirit of Lily hovering halfway between this world and the next, reflecting on the various aspects of her life. It seems that Lily was prepared to voice her own opinions, argue her point, but bite her tongue when needed. In the third poem we see the depth of Prior's grief and his awareness of the profound debt he owed her. She was light to his shade, and he clearly adored her. She managed the family on a small income and supported Prior's writing through good times and bad. I think her death hit Prior badly, only three years after saying goodbye to his eldest son. He had spent so many years searching for love, as his earliest poems from the 1870s reveal and had then found his soulmate in Lily. Her unswerving support had allowed him to follow his dream of being a writer. Now she was gone, and he would never be as happy again. After this he seems to have become more withdrawn and reclusive, unwilling to actively promote his work to the public and often feeling that his writing was undervalued by publishers and the literary establishment.

More tragedy was to follow. In September 1914 the Great War began in Europe. Many of the young men who had emigrated to Canada now answered the call to join up and help the old motherland. Walter enlisted in Winnipeg on 20th March 1916, joining the 78th Battalion, Canadian Infantry, Manitoba Regiment. On 26th October 1916 he sailed from Halifax on the *SS Grampian* and served on the Western Front in France. His regiment was in action straight away. The Bingham Heritage Trails Association website shows that during February and March 1917 he had three episodes of pneumonia and was hospitalised in the UK with three weeks convalescence at home. In March 1918 he was granted 2 weeks leave to the UK. Then, in August 1918:

'The 78th Battalion, known as The Winnipeg Grenadiers, were in action around Damery on 15-17th August.

Walter was wounded in the throat during the advance between Boves and Hallu during the overall advance from Amiens. Between 8th and 19th August the battalion was involved in Operation Llandovery Castle, so named to commemorate the torpedoing of the Canadian Hospital Ship on the 27th June. A typed report of the operation, which involved advancing through a number of villages beginning with Gentelles, 13 kilometres SE of Amiens, notes various actions on the way where Canadian soldiers were killed or wounded. Walter's medical records suggest he was wounded on the 9th when 3 officers and another 5 other ranks were wounded.

Medical record card: GSW Throat admitted to Canadian General Hospital Le Treport (near Dieppe) on August 9th. Dangerously ill on 18th (sic) then corrected on another card to died 17th.

His soldier's will stipulated that all his estate would be split equally between his sister Dorothy and brother Harold of The Banks, Bingham. They received Can$436.54 on 7/12/1918.'

Walter is buried at Mont Huon Military Cemetery, Le Treport, France. He is also commemorated on the headstone of Lily and James in Bingham Cemetery and appears on the Bingham Roll of Honour with the other young men of the town who fell in World War I.

The Mont Huon Cemetery where Walter Kirk is buried

Margaret, eldest of the Kirk children, qualified as a teacher sometime after the 1911 Census. We can pick her up in 1921 when she was an Assistant Mistress at the Gelligaer Intermediate School for Girls (now the Lewis Girls' Comprehensive), in Hengoed, South Wales. She appears again in the 1939 Register, still at the school and living alone in a comfortable terraced house in Hengoed. Margaret died a year later, on 2nd August 1940, aged 57 and is buried with Dorothy in a grave a few metres away from Lily and James in Bingham Cemetery.

Dorothy continued to stay at home and took over responsibility for the household after Lily's death. Harold was just a little boy, and she must have had to bring him up as well as caring for her distraught and often ailing father. We know from Stephen Fisher that Dorothy used to read to Prior when his eyes were bad. Harold died young in 1931, aged only 23. After that Dorothy was unable to keep on Banks Cottage. She had no professional qualifications and had spent most of her adult life caring for her family. In the 1939 Register she is listed as living at Porchester Terrace, Long Acre in Bingham. She was not the owner or tenant, so she must have been working as a live-in domestic, a housekeeper perhaps. We know she remained living in Bingham until her death in 1978 at 87 years old, but I have not been able to pin down her movements. All we know for certain is that none of the Kirk children married.

We know from Stephen Fisher's correspondence that Dorothy was keen to promote her father's work and memory after his death, supplying the Memorial Committee with material and giving Adelaide Wortley access to Prior's papers, including a photograph, for the entry on Prior in her 1954 *History of Bingham*. Dorothy gave Prior's poetry manuscripts to Fisher and attached loose sheets containing his last work, written just before his death, and then worked with Fisher to ensure that some of her father's papers found a home in the Nottinghamshire County Archives. On the headstone for Margaret and Dorothy's joint grave, they describe themselves as the '*daughters of James Prior Kirk*', clearly proud of their father's achievements to the end of their lives.

PRIOR AND THE ENGLISH DIALECT DICTIONARY

Prior's reputation up to now has rested on the novels, particularly *Forest Folk*, which makes him an interesting regional author of some ability and originality. In the course of my research, I came upon material which casts a whole new light on his work and in my opinion makes him an even more significant writer and amateur philologist.

Prior's use of the Nottinghamshire dialect was a feature of all his books, with the exception of *Hyssop*. On the whole, he uses dialect to define social class, just as Thomas Hardy, and later D.H. Lawrence, did. However, throughout his life he was systematically collecting, recording, and ordering words and phrases in the dialect of the Nottinghamshire countryside, especially the south of the county, the area where he lived. He was part of a national wave of interest that grew out of the Arts and Crafts movement, studying the traditional culture of ordinary people, which led to endeavours such as Cecil Sharpe's study of folk song and Iona and Peter Opie's work on the culture of childhood.

In Prior's case he was part of a monumental work of reference, *The English Dialect Dictionary*, which attempted to capture the dialects of the British Isles before they disappeared.

The English Dialect Dictionary was the brainchild of a remarkable man, Joseph Wright, a working-class boy from Bradford who only learnt to read at the age of 15. Still in his teens, he became fascinated with languages and attended night school to study French, German and Latin. He went on to study in Germany and Leeds and ended up as Professor of Comparative Philology at Oxford University. Wright had a strong interest in English dialects. Between 1898 and 1905 Wright produced *The English Dialect Dictionary* with the financial support of Professor W.W. Skeat, founder and president of the English Dialect Society, and A.J. Balfour (Prime Minister 1902-1905) who made a grant from the Royal Bounty Fund. The Dictionary was issued progressively in 28 parts, making up six volumes published in 1898, 1900, 1902, 1903, 1904, and 1905. *Mr. J.P. Kirk of Bingham* is listed as a 'Correspondent' and also as a 'Voluntary Reader'. His contributions can be found throughout the six volumes as a specialist in the words of South Nottinghamshire.

I have no idea how Prior became involved with this project, but I have discovered his working methods as he collected dialect.

In the Nottinghamshire County Archives, I found M/23089 *Correspondence and notes of James Prior Kirk concerning Nottinghamshire material in the English Dialect Dictionary.* This bundle consists of a few small postcards from the editors of the Dictionary asking for clarification of words and expressing thanks for contributions, for example: *'Can you kindly tell us the meaning of dog-dormer in your Forest Folk p.248'*. Clearly these are just a few remnants of what must have been a long series of exchanges. There are also rough lists of words, some ticked off, on scraps of paper. On its own, this bundle was intriguing but not very enlightening. My curiosity was aroused.

Then I opened M441 a small, thick book with a battered and well-worn cover. My first assumption was that this was Prior's personal Bible.

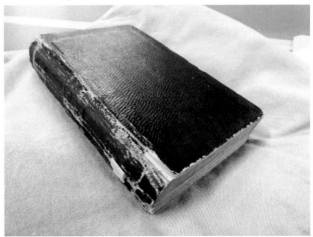

Then I opened it:

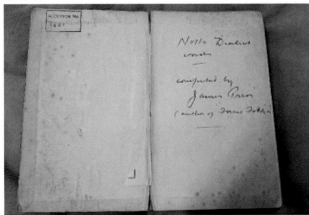

Notts Dialect words Compiled by James Prior (author of Forest Folk)

Turning through the many pages of this scruffy old notebook we can follow Prior as he travelled around the Nottinghamshire countryside, listening, noting down words and phrases, then sorting and indexing when he got home ready to send lists off to the Dictionary offices in Oxford or use them in his own writing. In the front of the book are his rough notes, some in pencil, some in pen, sometimes with the name of the person he was listening to – *Mrs Taylor, Mr B* etc, – pages and pages of his 'field notes', the handwriting often hard to decipher.

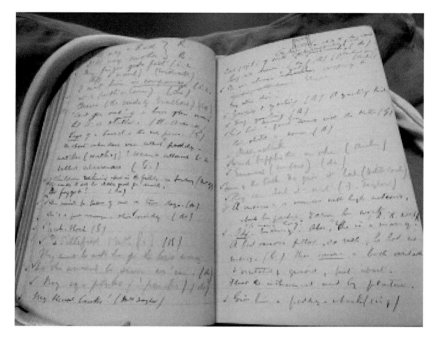

Turn the book over and start from the other end, and the words are arranged by letter of the alphabet so that they can be found quickly. The handwriting is much clearer, presumably done when he was sorting through his notes at home. I followed many entries through from the notebook to the pages of the *Dictionary* and then to Prior's own books. As well as contributing to the *Dictionary*, Prior was using his research to inform his own writing and to bring the language to life in the mouths of his characters. This combination of scientific collection and creativity makes him very special. Not only is the dialect recorded in a methodical, scientific manner, but it also has vitality, colour and energy in his books. Not even Thomas Hardy, also a 'correspondent' for the *Dictionary* for Dorset, or later D.H. Lawrence, managed to combine these qualities so spectacularly.

To take just one of many examples: I followed the word 'pedigree' from the index section of the notebook –

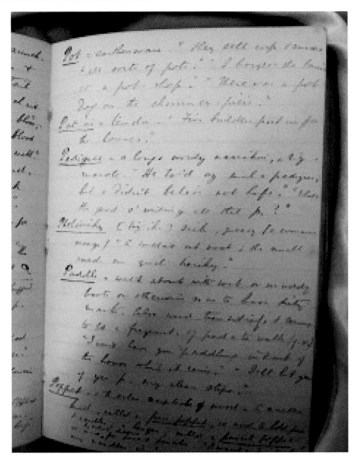

Pedigree a long wordy narration, a rigmarole.
"He told uz such a pedigree, but a didn't believe not hafe."
"Where's the good o' writing all that p.?"

Exactly the same words appear in the *Dictionary, Volume 4 page 452* under the entry 'Pedigree' with the attribution *'(J.P.K.)'* – this can be viewed online.[xvii]

Finally, in *A Walking Gentleman*, after a long-winded account by one of the more comic characters, his neighbour says: *'But what did 'e saäy after all that pedigree?'* – in other words, get to the point!

Prior used dialect in *Renie* and *Ripple and Flood*, published in 1895 and

1897, so it is possible that Wright came across Prior from those novels, but certainly 'J.P.K.' was actively contributing by the time the first volume was issued in 1898. The notebook was in use for many years – the Archive suggests c1890-1920. Unfortunately, the entries are not dated. However, the battered state of the cover suggests that it travelled with Prior, in his pocket or his knapsack, as he journeyed through the countryside gathering material for his novels.

The notebook also served as a working aide-memoir, with lists of addresses for publishers and periodicals, and has odd newspaper cuttings stuck in, with dialect words underlined.

If Prior had written no novels, his work as a collector of dialect would be reason enough to remember and honour him. This aspect of his work has been largely over-looked because the focus of articles about him has tended to be *Forest Folk* or its countryside settings. It is possible that a renewed interest in dialect will encourage more scholars to examine his contribution to our cultural and linguistic history and give this philological work the recognition that it deserves.

DECLINE AND DISAPPOINTMENT

Fortuna Chance was Prior's last published work. He completed two more novels, *November* and *Loosestrife,* but they failed to find a publisher, and the manuscripts are now lost. We know nothing about *November's* theme or location; *Loosestrife* was apparently set around the Trent valley village of Fiskerton, so perhaps he was trying to reprise the success of *Ripple and Flood.* He continued to write poetry and may have circulated a selection under the title *'Canticles' by Vacuus,* but again, publishers were not interested. His work had failed to hit the high spots of best seller status and literary tastes were changing. His narrative language, formal and Victorian, which Prior said he inherited from his father, was not the language of the new century. Prior seemed to belong to the past and no one was prepared to take another chance with him.

Prior hardly helped his cause. He was by nature quite an introvert and although he loved exploring the countryside of the East Midlands on his own and talking to people one to one, he was uncomfortable in crowds. Publishers expected authors to 'sell' their books and themselves – Dickens had shown how public readings could boost sales – so an author who was shy and uncooperative was not an attractive prospect. In terms of local interest there was a new Nottinghamshire writer emerging in the more energetic and newsworthy person of D.H. Lawrence. Modern, controversial, and also using the local voice, Lawrence perhaps benefited from coming after an author who had achieved some success using dialect. Lawrence's *The White Peacock* was published in 1911 by Heinemann, who had published *Forest Folk* ten years earlier. Lawrence was certainly aware of Prior's work. He wrote in a letter to Edward Garnett, writer and critic: *'What a curious man James Prior is! I did not know him, and he was so near home. I was very much interested. But what curious, highly flavoured stuff!'* In another letter he wrote: *'the whole household … has devoured James Prior, asking 'why is he a failure?' – Wm Heinemann said he was.'* Lawrence and Prior would have certainly shared their dissatisfaction with publishers. Prior, on the other hand, was not a fan of Lawrence's writing and commented *'We deal in different realities.'*[xviii]

Stephen Fisher felt that the Great War played a part: *'and in the clouds of battle the star of James Prior again suffered eclipse. The shadow of that eclipse was still over him when he died.'* Taste and fashions were changing.

Prior's personal tragedies, the deaths of Lily and Walter, must have contributed to his decline. His eye problems increased, and Fisher describes how at one of their meetings Prior was suffering from temporary blindness and said that *'"Dorothy has been reading* Forest Folk *to me. It is better than I thought it was. I didn't think I had it in me to write like that." He said this quite simply and modestly, as if he were apologising to his own work for having under-rated it.'*

Prior still had friends in the local literary world. The City Librarian, Walter Briscoe, admired Prior's books, especially *Forest Folk*. I suspect he knew about Prior's work for *The Dialect Dictionary* because he asked him to prepare some index cards as a glossary for his novels, for the library. In the autumn of 1919, he invited Prior to give a talk at the Nottingham Central Library. Prior's reply reveals both his shyness and self-deprecating sense of humour:

'I am greatly obliged to you for the kindness of your writing and of your attack upon the lethargy of my publishers. I wish I had a clear way of showing my appreciation of both. But to lecture! or even 'talk' publicly! A mild-mannered man like myself, only accustomed to raise his voice authoritatively in the bosom of his complacent family! Besides I have neither methodical knowledge of the subject matter nor practised skill in public speaking; and failing those qualifications I have not the necessary presumption to carry me through.

Or to preside! I who have never had any more important presidency than to be vice at a tea table. I simply shouldn't know how to do it. I know you will say that I should only have to stand and stutter; and as for the standing, probably in my blind eagerness to evacuate the platform I should plunge straight down among the audience, forgetful of orderly exit by the stairs. For in addition to my other disqualifications, my daylight half-sight is diminished to a bare quarter by night.

I think that in your proposal you were thinking of my interest much more than of yourself and your public. I hope you will not think me ungrateful. I have great desire to oblige you; and I am, with many thanks,

Yours very truly,

James P. Kirk [xix]

It must have been this reluctance to engage with the public that created the idea of a reclusive and disappointed author which has subsequently followed Prior through later appreciations of his work.

Other contemporary writers expressed their admiration for his work. J M Barrie wrote:

'I read 'A Walking Gentleman' with uncommon joy, often speak about it, am often spoken to about it. He is a fine writer, whose work I cherish.'

John Buchan, the author of *The 39 Steps*, said:

'I have the greatest possible admiration for James Prior's writing. He is the greatest modern novelist of the English Midlands.'

Some recognition did come his way in the form of a small, but very welcome, Civil Pension for Services to Literature. I find it hard to believe that Prior's limited success as a novelist would warrant such an award, so I wonder if it was his work on *The English Dialect Dictionary* that tipped the balance? Certainly, Balfour, one of its backers, was in a good position to recommend Prior. The money was welcome; Prior's income from his books declined sharply and by the time of his death the novels were no longer in print.

In March 1928, Stephen Fisher sent a letter to the *Nottingham Journal* describing his last meeting with Prior:

'Sir, I remember vividly the last occasion on which I saw James Prior. I had word from him that he was coming to Nottingham to see an eye doctor. I met him after his business had been done, and we walked up to my house, as was our custom on such occasions, for tea and an hour or two's companionship. We talked, I remember, about music. He appreciated good music, and in his early days, when living in Nottingham, had been fond of choir and glee-singing. He told me that one of the things he missed in his seclusion in Bingham was the opportunity of hearing good music. I played over a few gramophone records which I thought would interest him, and he sat by the fire making the toast while my wife was setting the tea-table. It was his nature to be helpful in little things. He seemed to be in a mood of wistful retrospection. It was not often that he talked about himself; but that afternoon he did, speaking from his own remembrance of the strange workings of the imagination of a child. Probably this came about because one of the records played and talked about was Schumann's Scenes of Childhood.

Suddenly, as if to excuse himself, he said: "I'm beginning to feel old. Play something jolly." Then I put on a Scotch reel played on the bagpipes, and in the middle of it he sprang up and danced a wild dance on the hearthrug, dramatically waving the toasting fork and toast above his head. His foot caught against some obstacle and down he sprawled in dangerous proximity to the fire, from which we rescued him, laughing and unharmed. He laid the blame of his downfall on his boots. "They're a new pair," he said, "and not exactly dancing shoes." They were not, but good, strong, tramping boots, hob-nailed. With a sudden return to wistfulness he said, "I don't suppose I shall wear them out."

Later, as I walked with him to the railway-station, he took my arm and leaned heavily on it as we went up hill. Again he whimsically blamed his boots. "But," he said, "they're the last pair I shall buy, so I must keep friends with them."

I have often wondered since whether his words were pure jest or veiled earnest. I little thought as I said goodbye to him that night that in a few weeks I should remember them as a prophecy sadly fulfilled.'

What a wonderful picture of Prior, happy and at ease in the home of a good and trusted friend.

In late November 1922, Prior caught a severe chill. It developed into pneumonia, and he died on 19th December aged 71. His last weeks were spent still writing poetry, pouring out his final thoughts with a sense of fatalism and acceptance, which to me shows that he knew the end was coming. Pasted into the back of his poetry manuscript, presumably by Dorothy, are his final poems. The first was written in July 1922 and revised in November:

I drop my tired eyelids, shut off the outer world,
Call in my wondering thoughts, revoke my vain desires,
Absent myself from all disquietudes,
Humble my spirit, refusing to the flesh,
So withdraw inwardly to God within me,
Bringing myself to the verge of nothingness,
(Myself, of such importance to myself)
To rest in a complete simplicity
Upon the lap of all-sufficiency,
Laying the burden of one upon the whole,
Surrendered to the infinite, universal indivisible love;
If I may catch, even so faintly, the all-wise suggestion,
If I may subject myself, even so imperfectly, to the great purpose,
If I may lose myself, even so grossly, in the all-pervading joy,
If – through so many ifs of mystery –
I may enlarge, restrain, perfect this me,
And bring it into oneness with the whole.

November 1922

What is a man?
A being who fain would keep his thoughts within the span
Of his material fingers;
Whose love lingers
About the things of touch and sound and sight.
He draws back in affright
From distance, depth and height:
Ever preferring a little to the whole,
He shades his eyes
Against the danger of a great surprise;
He shutters from the light
The mysteried recesses of his soul;
And in this craven mood
Leaves unexplored
The border campaigns of infinitude,
The wonder-shored.

12th November 1922

I would slip mortality's anchorage,
I let myself go from myself,
A little way, according to a man's strength;
Extending myself unto God without me,
With impossible irresistible endeavour
To discover the unmapped shores of infinity;
Losing myself if haply I could find Him;
Hoping at least that in this oceanic dip
I shall be washed clean of some clotted grossness,
Be humbled of some pride, strengthened in some weakness,
And so return into my inwardness
With clearer vision, purer understanding,
A simpler joy in being, a truer aim in doing.

This may be the last thing that Prior wrote. To me, it shows his deep spirituality and readiness to let the ambitions of his life go as he turned to God with faith in His mercy.

James Prior Kirk was buried in the cemetery at the eastern end of The Banks in Bingham. The old churchyard around the Anglican church was closed to further burials and a new cemetery opened on The Banks in 1888. This was much more acceptable as a final resting place for a Dissenting family like the Kirks. Lily was already resting there, so James joined her, later to be followed by their younger son Harold. Walter's death is also recorded on the headstone, although he is buried in France. A few yards away, lie Margaret and Dorothy.

The inscription on Prior's headstone reads:

In loving memory of
JAMES PRIOR KIRK
better known as JAMES PRIOR
Died Dec. 19th 1922 aged 71
Also his wife LILY
Died Mar 9th 1914 aged 48
Also of their sons
WALTER
Died of wounds in France Aug 17th 1918 aged 26
and HAROLD
Died Apr 25th 1931 aged 23

Prior's grave in Bingham Cemetery on The Banks

It's such a pity that Prior wasn't around to read his own obituaries; it would surely have cheered him up a great deal. The death of this quiet man, who had craved recognition, was announced by the *Nottingham Journal* on 20th December 1922:

JAMES PRIOR

The death of Mr. James Prior, the author of 'Forest Folk', takes from our midst one whom few have cared to honour, although his work merited full recognition and was esteemed by men of genius. Neither the University Colleges nor the City ever chose to pay him homage or even acknowledgment. But it is the way of cities and universities to honour those only who make a popular appeal, and not those whose genius is of a quiet intellectual order, having to be sought and requiring good taste to find it. It was ever thus.

Yet it may be James Prior felt himself honoured and recognised by the warm recognition which fell from the lips of so great a master as Sir James Barrie. The latter, after reading 'Forest Folk', declared that had he known James Prior was living in Nottingham at the time he, Sir James, was here – when editor of this paper – he would have knocked on every door until he had found him.

A quiet man, full of kindness, he has slipped out of life, but there remains of him that form of memorial which endures when princes are forgotten and mighty magnates dust.

In a further obituary the *Journal* wrote:

Nottinghamshire can congratulate itself that...he proved one of the very few novelists who have selected this county for the seat of their novels, which were mostly historical. His best known book is, of course, "Forest Folk", which deals with the Calverton and Annesley districts of the shire in the days of the Luddite riots, when the old-fashioned operatives bitterly resented the advent of mechanical frames. This novel, which practically reached the rank of a classic, made the name of "James Prior" familiar far beyond the confines of this county.

Skilled in the writing of Notts. dialect, in itself a difficult study if accuracy is to be maintained, other books which helped to popularise his name were "Fortuna Chance", which concerned itself with the beginnings of Methodism in Notts., and the Jacobite plots that were rife in the early days of the Hanoverian kings, "Ripple and Flood", "Renie" and "The Walking Gentleman". He also did a certain amount of miscellaneous writing.

At last, this unassuming man, who had been compared by reviewers to George Eliot, Dickens, Hardy and Scott, was getting the sort of plaudits he felt he deserved.

THE MEMORIAL COMMITTEE

Stephen Fisher remained a true friend to the end, and beyond. In the years following Prior's death, Fisher gathered support for some sort of permanent memorial to Prior. In 1927 he formed The James Prior Memorial Committee, with the aim of raising funds for a tangible memorial in Nottingham, and to bring out a new edition of *Forest Folk*. The Mayor, John Freckingham, the City Librarian, Walter Briscoe, and various other locally eminent figures all contributed. Over the next few years, Fisher was busy gathering support and funds, and lobbying publishers. In 1925 a cheap paper-cover edition was issued by the *Mansfield and Kirkby Chronicle*, printed on thin paper, in double columns, and designed to be cheap – 1s 6d – and accessible to the working people. Fisher wrote an introduction.

In 1927 the *Nottingham Journal* reported a further edition:

JAMES PRIOR
*Author of 'Forest Folk' a Nottinghamshire
classic which has just been published
by Cecil Palmer (3/6)*

The James Prior Memorial Committee and the publisher are alike to be congratulated on the fashion in which this epic of Sherwood Forest is once more made available to the reading public after having been out of print for some time. The merit of Prior's work, with its glowing colour of village life in the days of the Luddites, was fittingly extolled at the time of the Notts. Novelist's lamented death; it only remains here to express the hope that the enterprise of the committee and publisher will be rewarded by a ready demand for this new edition, which will perpetuate Prior's memory in worthy manner. As has previously been explained in our columns, the profits are to go to the dead novelist's family.

As far as a more concrete memorial goes, the building of a new pub in Blidworth provided an unlikely opportunity. Prior, of course, was a teetotaller and very much condemned the demon drink in his books. Tant is led astray in *Forest Folk* by drink, Eva in *Hyssop* is undone by an addiction to gin. Also in *Hyssop*, there is a family debate about the evils of alcohol, which Ira kicks off with *"what do you derive from your fatal addiction to the accursed draught?"* and then goes on to condemn it as the cause of all sorts of misery, poverty and broken homes. So Prior may have turned in his grave at the thought of a pub to be named after him. Fisher had to use all his skills of tact and diplomacy to dissuade the owner of the new pub away from the name 'The James Prior' and towards a compromise of 'The Forest Folk'. One room of the pub was devoted to Prior memorabilia and had some stained-glass windows depicting scenes from *Forest Folk*.

The Forest Folk pub in Blidworth

The pub is no longer there, but the site is still known as 'Forest Folk Corner' and there is a municipal planter with a commemorative plaque. The stained-glass windows were rescued when the pub was demolished and are now in the chapel of St. Andrew's Mission Hall in Blidworth. They depict the epic hunt from Blidworth, through Calverton and on towards Oxton, when Nell's beloved old horse dies and Arthur tries to comfort her.

The memorial committee also decided to commission a portrait of James Prior and engaged local artist N. Denholme Davis to produce one. Based on a studio photograph taken in old age, the portrait shows Prior against the landscape of the Blidworth area, clutching his hat and a rolled-up notebook. The unveiling was a grand affair, reported at length in the *Nottingham Journal* on 27th October 1928.

ART OF JAMES PRIOR
NOTTINGHAM HONOURS ITS TALENTED AUTHOR

CASTLE PAINTING
THE LORD MAYOR'S ELOQUENT TRIBUTE

"The painter, it seems to me, has dipped his brush in the very essence of the personality and spirit of James Prior."
This was the sincere tribute to the art of Mr. N. Denholm Davis which was paid by the Lord Mayor of Nottingham (Ald. E. Huntsman) when yesterday at the Castle Museum he unveiled a charming portrait in oils of the author of "Forest Folk".

SIR JAMES BARRIE
WIRES CONGRATULATIONS TO NOTTINGHAM

The picture was provided by the James Prior Memorial Fund and is to have a permanent place in the Castle collection.

Ald. E.L. Manning (chairman of the Castle Museum committee), who presided, read this telegram from Sir James Barrie:-

"Congratulations to Nottingham on the honour it is doing itself by recognising the worth of James Prior." – J.M. Barrie

Among the company were the novelist's two daughters, Miss Margaret Kirk and Miss Dorothy Kirk.

That was a day, said the Lord Mayor, when lovers of the works of James Prior could rejoice at achieving the purpose which they set out to realise about eighteen months ago. James Prior deserved a place in the memory and affections of Nottingham and the district, and it would have been an eternal disgrace had they not recognised their duty to posterity by securing that they should have some memorial of their assessment of his value.

Nature Symbolised

To him, personally, the picture brought great satisfaction and delight because he felt that those who came after them would, when their eyes lit upon that picture, see and know James Prior. He was delighted by the accessories, the setting, the symbolism of the canvas, the hedgerows, the bushes and the uplands.

Were they not the scenes which the author loved? Were they not the setting in which he placed the creatures of his fancy in the books which he had left them?

After referring to other incidental but important touches in the portrait, the hat and the notebook held in the author's hands, the speaker said that the face itself was that of James Prior. It was never his privilege to meet him in the flesh, but from the accounts which he had had of him from the novelist's many friends he could see in that picture exactly what they had told him.

Seeing the Man

There was the quiet humour that floated about the eyes, the tender sympathy with the humble beings he described and made to live for them. His nature, his tender sympathy had been caught and beautifully expressed by the artist in that presentiment of the author.

The speaker paid tribute to those of the committee who had worked to bring about the setting up of that memorial. They were to be congratulated because they had performed a duty to the memory of James Prior, and to those who would come after them. It was right that they who read the pages which would never be allowed to perish, should have an opportunity of looking at the man.

Labour of Love

Mr. W.A. Briscoe (acting chairman of the Memorial Committee), proposing a vote of thanks to the Lord Mayor said that the committee had succeeded in getting "Forest Folk" published in a popular edition.

Mr. S. Fisher (a representative on the committee of the novelist's family) seconded the vote and the chairman was thanked on the proposition of Mr. H. Betts.

"The painting of this picture has been a labour of love," said Mr. Denholm Davis, who was only persuaded to speak "under orders" of the Lord Mayor. "With all my heart I have tried to put into it those sweet things that I have found in his books. I have tried to put into his features that sweet nature which he must have possessed."

The portrait is now in the care of Nottingham Central Library.

PRIOR'S LEGACY

In the years after Fisher's Memorial Committee, Prior was never completely forgotten. His novels went out of print, but they could still be found in the Nottingham City Central Library and at Bromley House members' Library. Occasional articles appeared in the magazine *The Nottinghamshire Countryside* where the emphasis was usually on the locations of his books, especially *Forest Folk*. Arthur Mee, in *The King's England, Nottinghamshire, The Midland Stronghold* (1938) waxed lyrical about him, writing *"James Prior Kirk wrote delightfully of the manners and customs of the old forest in Forest Folk"*. However, economic Depression, another World War, and a changed society all made Prior's books seem dated and irrelevant.

A century on from his death, however, things look rather different. Although he is very much a late Victorian writer in style, his themes have even more resonance today than they had when he was writing. His strong women – Ivy Sivil, Nell Rideout, Lady Sally, Fortuna Chance – are remarkably modern and would hold their own in any present-day television drama. Lord Beiley's journey of self-discovery, aided by people with very different life experiences, fits well with modern notions of equality and personal growth. Prior's tolerance and offer of opportunities to redeem misdeeds is more in line with our own ideas of rehabilitation rather than condemnation.

Prior has often been described as a writer of historical novels. In fact, only *Forest Folk* and *Fortuna Chance* have an historical backdrop. Certainly, in the latter, the influence of Sir Walter Scott can be felt, and even a touch of John Buchan, but Prior was always more interested in creating a good story with his own characters rather than re-interpreting history.

Nottingham and Nottinghamshire have always been a breeding ground for writers, and that great heritage was recognised when Nottingham became a UNESCO City of Literature in 2015. The lost writers of Notts are being steadily re-discovered and brought back to life. Rowena Edlin-White and John Baird have produced fascinating books introducing readers to a wide range of writers, novelists, poets and dramatists, old and new, and their locations in the landscape of the county.[xx] There is a renewed interest in regional dialect from academics and popular writers, and even Radio 4 now has a series called 'Tongue and Talk: the Dialect Poets' featuring current writers using dialect.[xxi]

Forest Folk was re-published by Leen Editions (Spokesman Books) in 2017 and there is hope that more of Prior's work may soon reach a wider audience. In his day he was compared with George Eliot, R.D. Blackmore, Sir Walter Scott and even Dickens, and was spoken of as 'the Thomas Hardy of Nottinghamshire', but his work never quite achieved their popular acclaim or longevity. His poetry was certainly not great, but it does provide an insight into his mind and heart and brings him to life. He remains a significant figure if only for his wonderful portrayals of life in the East Midlands countryside and for his work recording the language of its people.

In the year of the centenary of his death, Bingham will at last honour its most important literary figure with memorial 'blue plaques' on the two cottages where he lived and wrote, Lushai Cottage and Banks Cottage. Hopefully, this will encourage a few more people to seek out information about him and maybe even to read *Forest Folk*.

I set out to see what could be learnt about James Prior, or *'Mr Kirk of Bingham'* as I found pencilled onto the title page of a first edition of *Fortuna Chance*. I discovered not a sober recluse, but three versions of a complex man. First, a romantic but deeply conflicted young man, torn between filial duty to his family and his overwhelming desire to be a writer, trying and failing to keep the family business afloat, standing up to his father and doggedly pursuing his dream. Then, a husband and father, saved by Lily, the love of his life, who gave him a happy family life in Bingham and the encouragement to produce his best work. Finally, in his later years, a man weighed down by sorrow and disappointment, but still able to enjoy the company of a close friend, make toast by the fire and dance a reel until he fell over.

Prior left us very little evidence from which to reconstruct his life. I have tried to piece together the fragments, but in the end, it is the novels which can tell us most about this thoughtful and private man. His novels may seem rooted in the past but they still speak to us about equality and cooperation between the sexes and classes, tolerance, compassion and forgiveness, all messages with as much relevance today as ever. Let Prior himself have the last word:

"I have put the best of myself into my books,
they are me and nobody else."

NOTES

i. Forward by Stephen Fisher to the *Mansfield and Kirkby Chronicle* paperback edition of *Forest Folk* (1925)

ii. Stephen Fisher, *James Prior,* for *The Bookman* November 1917, Nottingham Central Library, Local Studies

iii. *Poems by James Prior*, 1925, collected by Stephen Fisher, Bromley House Library

iv. Jean Annabel Cooper, *James Prior – an Appreciation*, 1965, *Nottinghamshire Countryside* magazine, Vol. 26 No. 1, Nottingham City Archives.

v. James Prior, *Canticles by Vacuus* manuscript, Nottinghamshire County Archives M/16206

vi. The Band of Hope Union is mentioned in the Log Book of the new County School, October 1910, organising a conference for teachers about Temperance. (County Archives)

vii. http://www.nottshistory.org.uk/articles/sneinton/sm35_16-21.htm

viii. www.myprimitivemethodists.org.uk/content/chapels/nottingham

ix. Fisher, S., *James Prior* 1925, The James Prior Memorial Committee, Nottingham University, East Midlands Collection.

x. www.britishnewspaperarchive.co.uk and for all subsequent newspaper quotes

xi. http://tonyshaw3.blogspot.com/jamesprior

xii. William, 5th Baron Byron, 1722-1798, great uncle of the poet, Captain in the Duke of Kingston's Regiment against the Jacobite rebellion. He was known for his dissolute and violent life which included killing his cousin, William Chaworth, in a dispute at the Star & Garter Inn, Pall Mall over who had more game on their estates. He was tried for murder but found guilty of the lesser charge of manslaughter and paid a small fine. He was also thought to be a satanist, murderer and to have held orgies at his Newstead residence.

xiii. Jane Eyre says: "Women are supposed to be very calm generally; but women feel just as men feel; they need exercise for their faculties, and a field for their efforts as much as their brothers do."

xiv. Fisher, S., *James Prior* 1925, The James Prior Memorial Committee, in the collection of Nottingham University, East Midlands Collection.

xv. Hemstock, V. *Victorian Bingham*, published by Bingham Heritage Trails Association

xi. http://tonyshaw3.blogspot.com/jamesprior

xvii. https://archive.org/details/englishdialectdi06wriguoft

xviii. http://tonyshaw3.blogspot.com/jamesprior

xix. DD/1349/2 and 1349/18 Nottinghamshire County Archives, letter and transcript.

xx. Rowena Edlin-White, *Exploring Nottinghamshire Writers* 2017, Five Leaves Publications and John Baird, *Follow the Moon and the Stars: A Literary Journey through Nottinghamshire*, 2021, Five Leaves Publications

xxi. For example: Natalie Braber, *Pit talk of The East Midlands,* 2017, Bradwell Books; Scollins & Titford, *Ey Up Mi Duck: Dialect of Derbyshire and the East Midlands*, 2000, Countryside Books; David Crystal, *The Disappearing Dictionary: a Treasury of Lost English Dialect Words*, 2015, Pan Books

PICTURE REFERENCES

Cover picture and page 51 – NTGM011991 @picturenottingham.co.uk

Page 9 – Lushai Cottage, Photo: Ailish D'Arcy

Page 12 – Hoveringham 1900: NTGM017153 @picturenottingham.co.uk. The scene today, Photo: Ailish D'Arcy

Page 15 – The Banks 1909: binghamheritage.org.uk. Banks Cottage now, Photo: Ailish D'Arcy

Page 27 – Hyssop and the Wesleyan school, Photo: Ailish D'Arcy

Page 28 – Old Methodist Church,with the permission of Val Hemstock.

Page 29 – Primitive chapel, Photo: Ailish D'Arcy

Page 33 – Mont Huon: www.cwgc.org

Pages 36-38 – Photo: M441 Inspire Nottingham Archives

Page 45 – Photo: Ailish D'Arcy

Page 48 – Forest Folk Hotel: NTGM020735 @picturenottingham.co.uk/ Planter: tonyshaw3.blogspot.com

Page 49 – Window, Photo: Ailish D'Arcy

ACKNOWLEDGMENTS

My thanks go to John Smith, who writes as John Baird, for starting me off on this project, Tony Simpson of Spokesman Books for encouragement, Rowena Edlin-White, Geoff Ashton and the Bingham Heritage Trails Association, the local studies librarians at the Nottingham Central Library, the helpful staff at Nottinghamshire County Archives, and Professor Natalie Braber at Nottingham Trent University for giving up her time to talk to me about dialect. Manuscripts and Special Collections at the University of Nottingham include papers relating to James Prior.

PRIOR'S BOOKS

Forest Folk is the only novel so far available in a current edition – Leen Editions 2017 (available from www.spokesmanbooks.org).

Nottingham City Central Library has the full set of novels, except *Renie*. Bromley House members subscription Library in Nottingham has copies of all except *Renie*. It also has the small pamphlet of Prior's Poems published by Stephen Fisher and the Memorial Committee.

Facsimile reprints can be found online at abebooks.co.uk including the British Library's edition of *Renie*.